D1203633

1. An M10 rests by Ormoc Bay while the crew keeps an eye on a nearby burning Japanese barge. The M10s in the Philippines were used mainly to provide fire support for infantry units.

TANKS ILLUSTRATED No 19

US TANK DESTROYERS
of World War Two

STEVEN J. ZALOGA

ARMS AND ARMOUR PRESS

Introduction

Published in 1985 by Arms and Armour Press,
2–6 Hampstead High Street, London NW3 1QQ.

Distributed in the United States by
Sterling Publishing Co. Inc., 2 Park Avenue,
New York, N.Y. 10016.

British Library Cataloguing in Publication Data:
Zaloga, Steven J.
US tank destroyers of World War Two. – (Tanks
illustrated; no. 19)
1. Tanks (Military science) – United States –
History   2. World War, 1939–1945 – Tank warfare
I. Title   II. Series
623.74′752′0973   UG446.5
ISBN 0-85368-770-6

Editing, design and artwork by Roger Chesneau.
Typesetting by Typesetters (Birmingham) Ltd.
Printed in Italy by Tipolitografia G. Canale
& C. S.p.A., Turin, in association with Keats
European Ltd.

In the wake of the unexpected defeat of France in 1940 at the hands of the German panzer divisions, the US Army was in a quandary regarding its anti-tank doctrine. As a result of peacetime manoeuvres, the Army Ground Forces under Gen. L. McNair developed a curious doctrine which would guide US armoured vehicle development through the war. This doctrine envisaged tanks acting in defensive support of infantry, and in the offensive roles of exploitation and breakthrough. Tanks were not to be used to fight enemy tanks; rather, the latter would be dealt with by another weapon entirely, the tank destroyer.

Tank destroyers were seen as being wheeled or tracked vehicles, better armed and faster than tanks but more thinly armoured; they would hunt out enemy tanks, engaging them from hidden positions where their lack of protection would not make them too vulnerable. This doctrine contrasted sharply with that of the Germans, who although they eventually built lightly armoured tank destroyers (panzerjägers) did not do so primarily by choice but rather because of economic exigency: Germany had many obsolete light tanks which could be put to better use as panzerjägers. However, German doctrine always assumed that tanks would be the primary enemy of other tanks, and so German tanks were armed accordingly.

American tank destroyer development was at first both hasty and confused. Some of the early designs were faulty and, unfortunately, entered combat service to the risk of their crews. Later, in the North African campaign, the first M10 tank destroyers became available; these would become the primary weapons of the armoured tank destroyer battalions. (There were also towed tank destroyer battalions, which used a variety of towed anti-tank guns.) The first serious encounters with large amounts of German armour came in 1944 in France, and American tanks like the M4 Sherman proved to be woefully undergunned since Army doctrine presumed that tank destroyers would deal with German tanks. There were never enough tank destroyers to do so. Fortunately, by a combination of air superiority, shortages in German equipment and tactical skill, the armoured divisions circumvented this problem, and except in the Battle of the Bulge German armour did not appear in significant numbers after the autumn of 1944. Tank destroyer battalions indeed served with distinction in the European campaign, their crews often displaying common sense to overcome the shortcomings in their equipment, but the Army eventually realized how short-sighted their tank destroyer doctrine had been, and after the war it was dropped and the tank destroyer battalions were disbanded.

This book is intended to provide a pictorial guide to the varied equipment used by the armoured tank destroyer battalions of the US Army during the Second World War in both the European and Pacific theatres. The photographs are almost all drawn from US Army Signal Corps files located at the Pentagon, the National Archives, DAVA, and the Fort Knox Patton Museum.

Steven Zaloga

◀2
2. An M10, supported by troops of the 10th
Mountain Division, gingerly makes its way up a
narrow mountain road in the Cartel Di Angelo area,
3 March 1945.

▲3

▲4   ▼5

3. The alternative to tank destroyers: infantry practise anti-tank tactics against a dummy Japanese Type 89 tank at Camp Hood in 1943.

4. In the late 1930s and early 1940s the US Army began experiments with open-turreted tank destroyers which used larger guns than their tank counterparts – in this case, a 37mm gun in lieu of the machine guns usually carried on this M2A1 light tank.

5. The defeat of France in 1940 brought about a great deal of US interest in motorized anti-tank equipment. Much was improvised, this combination of a standard Army M3A1 37mm anti-tank gun and a jeep (Camp Funston, November 1941), being an example.

6. The Camp Funston tank destroying jeep's main problem was that the chassis was too light even for so small a gun as the 37mm.

7. Another improvised tank destroyer was this curious attempt mounted on a Swamp Buggy at Fort Meade in August 1941.

▲8   ▼9

8

8. The T14 project, one of the Army's first serious attempts to develop a tank destroyer on the basis of a jeep.
9. The second pilot version of the T14 jeep tank destroyer, heavily modified at the rear to make the gun more accessible.
10. Another view of the T14 tank destroyer during trials at Fort Meade in September 1941.
11. On the T14 the vehicle stowage was moved to a special bin on the front side.
12. The T21 was a more sophisticated jeep tank destroyer, employing a double truck axle at the rear to provide more support for the gun while firing. An improved shield was also fitted.

10▲

11▲   12▼

▲13 ▼14

13. One of the final jeep tank destroyer attempts was the T44, which mated a heavily modified jeep with a 57mm anti-tank gun.

14. One of the truly dreadful tank destroyers was the M5 75mm Gun Motor Carriage. This monstrosity, mating a 75mm gun on an Air Force Cletrac runway towing tractor, was actually type-classified. The crews dubbed it 'Cleak-Track', and someone in the Army procurement department came to his senses before it was produced in quantity.

15. The outcome of the many attempts to produce a jeep tank destroyer was the M6 37mm Gun Motor Carriage, which married the 37mm gun with a Dodge ¾-ton light truck in lieu of a jeep. It was among the first tank destroyers to enter service, in 1942. This vehicle was photographed at Camp Chaffee.

16. An overhead view of the M6 GMC. The gun was supposed to be fired over the rear, and the vehicle could then escape to another hiding position to fire.

◄ 16

▲17

17. A flamboyant display using the M6 GMC's weapons, during the 1942 Tennessee manoeuvres.

18. The new M6, seen during manoeuvres in Arkansas in November 1942, about the same time it was entering combat in North Africa.

19. When the M6 first entered action with the tank destroyer battalions in North Africa it proved extremely unpopular, owing partly to its lack of armour and partly to the relative ineffectiveness of its 37mm gun. Most were withdrawn from service in short order and converted back to light trucks.

20. An M6 37mm GMC in North Africa in 1943 before being decommissioned into a truck.

21. The 37mm gun from an M6. Some of these weapons were later mounted in M2 half-tracks by the 2nd Armoured Division.

▲18   ▼19

▲22

22. The first successful tank destroyer design was the T12, which combined the M3 halftrack with a modernized version of the French 75mm 'soixante-quinze' gun of First World War fame. The photograph shows a T12 on exercise at Camp Hood in 1942.

23. When the T12 was type-classified for service use it became the M3 75mm Gun Motor Carriage (GMC), GMC being the official ordnance designation for tank destroyers. This T12 (M3) GMC is seen at Camp Hood in 1942.

▼ 23

24. A rare view of the first operational use of the M3 75mm GMC. In 1941 fifty of these vehicles were shipped to the Philippines where they formed the three battalions of the Provisional Field Artillery Brigade. This photograph shows an M3 GMC knocked out in 1942.

In the Pacific, the M3 75mm GMC was popularly called the SPM (Self-Propelled Mount).
25. The standard production model of the M3 GMC had a new shield which offered more protection to the gun crew.

▲26 ▼27

26. An M3 75mm GMC engages an M3 medium tank at point-blank range during July 1942 exercises at Camp Hood.
27. An M3 GMC crew displays its small-arms firepower during the October 1942 Tennessee manoeuvres.
28. A clear view of the new shield on the production model M3 75mm GMC, this vehicle belonging to the 802nd Tank Destroyer (TD) Battalion at Boonesville, Virginia, April 1943.
29. A grim reminder of the inadequacies of the lightly armoured tank destroyers when faced by tank: M3 GMCs knocked out by German tanks in Tunisia during the 1943 fighting.

28▲   29▼

17

▲ 30

30. The experiences of M3 GMCs in North Africa were mixed. When properly employed they could be effective, but their technical shortcomings and their tactical misuse generally rendered them ineffective. Here French troops practise on an M3 GMC.
31. Although the M3 GMC was phased out of front-line Army service after the campaigns in Tunisia and Sicily, it remained in use in the Pacific theatre. Each Marine division had twelve assigned to its Special Weapons Battalion, with which the vehicle saw service through to 1945.

▼ 31

32 ▲

32. Marine SPMs saw occasional anti-tank fighting (as at Saipan in 1944) but were used mainly to attack bunkers.

33. One of the least known tank destroyers developed by the US Army was the T48 57mm GMC produced specifically for the British Army. By the time it was ready, however, the 57mm gun was outdated, and most of the T48s were given to the Soviet Union. In the Soviet Army they were known as SU-57s, and several are seen here entering the Old City of Prague in May 1945. (CTK via Jiri Hornat)

33 ▼

▲34　▼35

34. The M10 consisted of a 3in gun mounted on a modified M4 Sherman tank chassis and first entered combat in North Africa in 1943. This particular M10 3in GMC, photographed at Oran in 1943, has one of the later-style rear turret counter-weights.

35. Another example of the M10 tank destroyer at Oran in 1943. The M10 soon became the most common tank destroyer type in the American battalions, replacing both the M3 GMC and the M6 GMC.

36. A pair of initial production M10 tank destroyers in Tunisia in 1943, showing the early-style rear turret counterweight.

37. An M10 tank destroyer of the 899th TD Battalion during the fighting near Maknassy in April 1943. The 899th had done well in earlier fighting at El Guettar during the first combat engagements of the M10.

◀**37**

▲38

38. An M10 at the Desert Training Center in 1943.

39. The main weakness of the M10 was its open turret, which made it vulnerable to overhead artillery bursts, small-arms fire and hand grenades. Here a TD crew practises anti-aircraft drill at Camp Carson, May 1943.

40. An M10 crew of the Tank Destroyer School at Camp Hood ride their vehicle, named 'Pistol Packin' Mama', during exercises in October 1943. Note the large black panther (the symbol of the tank destroyer force) painted on the rear turret counterweight.

41. An M10 tank destroyer in travel order in the Cassino region of Italy, 6 November 1943. In Italy the few tank targets meant that tank destroyers were often used for artillery support rather than in their intended role.

▼39

▲42 ▼43

42. An M10 of the 601st TD Battalion at the Anzio beach-head, 29 February 1944.
43. An M10 TD during operations in the Po Valley in March 1945. In the background is an incomplete Bailey bridge.

44. M10s of the 894th TD Battalion being used in the indirect artillery fire support role near Littoria, Italy, 18 March 1944.
45. An M10 passes a burnt-out Sherman tank near Littoria, Italy, 1 April 1944.

▲46

▲47   ▼48

46. M10s bypass a Tiger I tank they have knocked out near Cisterna, Italy, 25 May 1944.
47. From a smouldering battlefield, a T2 (M31) armoured recovery vehicle removes a disabled M10 tank destroyer. In the background are a wrecked German halftrack and a PzKpfw IV tank.
48. An M10 in action on the streets of Rome, 4 June 1944.

49. An M10 enters Rome on 5 June 1944. This particular M10 has had a sand-bag parapet added around the vulnerable roof opening.
50. M10s of the 710th TD Battalion, 1st Armored Division, fire at German positions across the Arno river, 25 August 1944.

49 ▲   50 ▼

▲51 ▼52

53▶

51. A good example of an M10 from the 804th TD Battalion engaging in artillery fire near Coiano, Italy, 7 October 1944.
52. The full extent of the use of these M10s as improvised artillery is evident from the number of spent shell casings and packing tubes that litter their positions near Sabbioni, Italy, 8 October 1944.

These M10s belonged to 'Able' Company, 804th TD Battalion.
53. An M10 tank destroyer rests near some cliffs outside the wrecked town of Livergnano, Italy, where local families have taken shelter, 19 October 1944.

▲54 ▼55

54. Infantry troops accompany an M10 of the 601st TD Battalion during the 1944 fighting.
55. The M10 tank destroyer was supplied to many armies under Lend-Lease. Here M10s of the 6th South African Division's 1/11 AT Regiment fire on German positions near Porretta, Italy, 17 November 1944.

56. South African M10 tank destroyers rest in hull defilade near Porretta, November 1944. These vehicles also belonged to 1/11 AT Regiment.
57. A camouflage-painted M10 of a TD battalion of the 5th Army fires during a night action in Italy, 20 February 1945.

▲58 ▼59

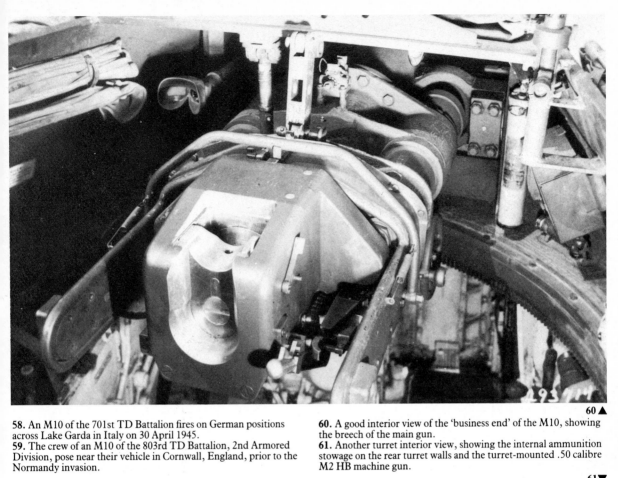

60 ▲

58. An M10 of the 701st TD Battalion fires on German positions across Lake Garda in Italy on 30 April 1945.
59. The crew of an M10 of the 803rd TD Battalion, 2nd Armored Division, pose near their vehicle in Cornwall, England, prior to the Normandy invasion.

60. A good interior view of the 'business end' of the M10, showing the breech of the main gun.
61. Another turret interior view, showing the internal ammunition stowage on the rear turret walls and the turret-mounted .50 calibre M2 HB machine gun.

61 ▼

▲62   ▼63

62. A view showing the third style of rear turret counterweight used on later production M10s. This version also had a slightly modified rear turret shape.

63. An M10 passes through St. Fromond in Normandy, 7 July 1944. A censor has obliterated the unit designator on the transmission housing.

64▲   65▼

64. An M10 fires on German positions during the fighting at St. Lo on 20 July 1944, part of the famous break-out operations. This M10 still has the wading trunk fitted at the rear which helped it get ashore at Normandy. The white smear is a censor's mark to cover the unit designator on the vehicle's rear.

65. An M10 presses ahead through the boscage country of St. Lo in Normandy, 24 July 1944. Notice that even at this early date crews were adding sand-bag armour to compensate for the vehicle's shortcomings.

66. An M10 passes through Percy, France, on 1 August 1944 following the successful American break-out.
67. An M10 rests in a peaceful French street following the Allied landings in southern France, August 1944.
68. An M10 named 'Babs' of the 5th Armored Division comes ashore at Dreaux in southern France during the landings there in August 1944.

▲66

▲67   ▼68

69. An M10 supporting
the 45th Division crosses
the Durance river in
France, 20 August 1944.
70. Infantry and tank
destroyers advance
through the suburbs of
Paris on 23 August 1944
in support of the French
2nd Armoured Division.
71. An M10 supporting
the 7th Division passes
through a column of
wrecked trucks in
Montelimar, 30 August
1944.

69 ▲

70 ▲   71 ▼

▲72 ▼73

74 ▲

72. The crew of an M10 clear rubble off their vehicle after German shelling. Note the helmet souvenir on the front headlight cover.
73. An M10 prepared for action, complete with a mascot attached to the front headlight bracket. Note that the crew have shed their official (but unarmoured) tanker's helmets in favour of the more practical and protective GI steel 'pot'.

74. Troops of the 22nd Infantry Regiment ride towards Mabompre, Belgium, 8 September 1944. This M10 still carries part of its wading trunk on the rear.
75. An M10 fires across the German border during the fighting on 14 September 1944.

75 ▼

▲76 ▼77

76. M10s of 'Able' Company, 634th TD Battalion, pass warily through the outskirts of Aachen, Germany, during the fighting there on 14 October 1944.

77. An M10 of the 645th TD Battalion nestles in the edges of the Vosges Forest near St. Benoit, France, 31 October 1944. Note that, by this time, improvised cover for the top roof opening was beginning to be added to tank destroyers in France.

78. This close-up photograph shows the early-style counter-weight on the turret of an M10 of the 601st TD Battalion in Brouvelieures, France, 4 November 1944. The yellow square with red 'Y' was the insignia of the 601st TD Battalion.

79. An M10 of the 893rd TD Battalion passes through the Huertgen Forest near Schmidt, Germany, during the bloody fighting there on 4 November 1944.

◀78

79▼

80. 'The Duke of Paduka', an M10 of the 712th TD Battalion, passes through Metzervisse, Germany, on 17 November 1944. In the background is an M4 (76mm) Sherman tank supporting the 90th Division.
81. An M10 supports an infantry advance past a barber's shop in the streets of Niederbronn-les-Bains in the Alsace region of France, 10 December 1944. Tank destroyers were not well suited to urban fighting like this owing to the vulnerability of their open turrets to grenades tossed from high windows.
82. An M10 of the 645th TD Battalion crushes its way past a road obstruction in Lembach, France, during the 7th Army's advance, 14 December 1944.
83. Men of the 331st Infantry Regiment warm themselves near the fire of a crew from the 629th TD Battalion outside Courtil, Belgium, on 20 January 1945 during the Ardennes fighting.
84. An M10 cautiously peers around the corner of a building in Habkirchen, Germany, while supporting the 35th Division of Patton's Third Army, 15 December 1944. Within a few days the armoured units of the Third Army would be hustling their way north to relieve American forces trapped in Bastogne during the Battle of the Bulge.
85. A good example of the type of improvised overhead cover added to many tank destroyers in 1944 and 1945 to offer some protection against snipers and overhead artillery bursts. This particular M10 belonged to the 813th TD Battalion and was photographed on 14 January 1945.

▲80   ▼81

▼82

83 ▲

84▲   85▼

86. The M10s of the 773rd TD Battalion had knocked out 103 German tanks up until the time this photograph was taken, this particular tank destroyer having accounted for five itself. The top battalion score in the ETO was 105 tanks, the average being 34.

87. A snow-covered M10 of the 636th TD Battalion provides anti-tank protection for the 36th Division near Bischwiller, France, 28 January 1945. By this time the M10 could deal with the German PzKpfw IV tank but was not capable of defeating the thicker front armour of the Panther and the Tiger.

86 ▶

▼87

◀89

88. A detailed view of the overhead armour developed by the 536th Ordnance HM Company and fitted to tank destroyers of the 7th Army in February 1945.

89. An M10 supporting the 8th Infantry Division passes through Duren, France, 24 February 1945. Surprisingly, it is still fitted with the Cullin hedgerow prongs which were added to some tanks and armoured vehicles in July 1944 during the break-out operations to help movement through the thick boscage of the Normandy region.

▲90 ▼91

90. An M10 passes the shell-pocked church in Rohrwiller, France, while supporting the attacks of the 36th Division, 4 February 1945.
91. A heavily stowed M10 fires over the Sauer river near Echternach, Luxembourg, during the fighting there on 7 February 1945.

92. An M10 moves through Jülich, Germany before entering an infantry assembly area prior to an attack outside the town on 24 February 1945.
93. An M10 of the 823rd TD Battalion passes through the ruins of Magdeburg, Germany, on 18 April 1945.

▲94 ▼95

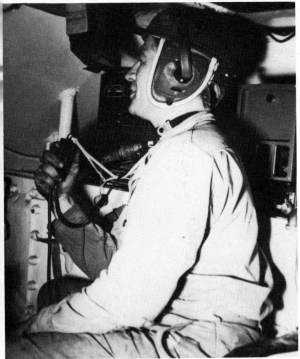

96 ▲

97 ▲

94. Another view of the type of overhead armour developed by the 536th Ordnance HM Co. for modifying M10 tank destroyers of the Seventh Army.

95. The crew of an M10 of the 632nd TD Battalion in Australia hold an impromptu meeting on the turret floor. The normal turret crew was three, and the two guests are the driver and co-driver who would normally sit in the front section of the hull.

96. A view of the co-driver's station in the M10. The co-driver had a set of driving controls, but his main responsibility was to man the vehicle radio.

97. A view of the driver of an M10 handling the large controls of his vehicle.

98. M10s were attached to the 767th Tank Battalion during the fighting on Kwajalein Island on 3 February 1944. Normally a tank battalion had M7 HMCs attached for fire support, but for the Kwajalein Atoll fighting the 767th had a platoon of M10s instead.

98 ▼

▲ 99

99. An M10 supporting the 77th Division in north-west Leyte during the Philippines fighting in 1945. Three tank destroyer battalions were used in the Philippines, but saw very little anti-tank fighting.

100. An interesting overhead view of the M18 Hellcat 76mm GMC. The M18 was the first custom-built tank destroyer and, capable of about 45mph, was the fastest armoured vehicle in US service during the Second World War. It was popular for both its speed and its firepower, although by the time it entered service in 1944 its gun was already inadequate to deal with Panther and Tiger tanks. This is one of the later production M18s with a muzzle brake on the gun tube.

101. M18s supporting the 91st Division enter Fonteloona, Italy, 11 September 1944.

102. An M18 rests in the ruins of the outskirts of Brest, France, 12 September 1944.

▼ 100

101▲ 102▼

▲103

103. The low, sleek lines of the M18 are very evident in this view. The M18 was undoubtedly preferred to the M10 by tank destroyer crews, although by the autumn of 1944 most would have liked a vehicle with a bigger gun or more armour – or both. This vehicle was photographed in Brest on 12 September 1944.

104. An M18 covers a road junction in Frambois, France, 22 September 1944.

105. An M18 Hellcat in Immendorf, Germany, on 11 December 1944. Because of the cramped conditions inside, the M18 had extensive stowage racks fitted to the exterior of the turret.

▲104 ▼105

106. An M18 of the 602nd Tank Destroyer Battalion fires on German positions near St. Goar, Germany, 26 March 1945. By the war's end the M18 equipped 23 of the tank destroyer battalions formed (almost 40 per cent), but far more M10-equipped battalions saw combat.

107. An M18 advances past the outskirts of Irsch, Germany, 27 February 1945.

108. A heavily marked M18 of the 824th TD Battalion fires in support of the 100th Division in fighting near Wiesloch, Germany, 1 April 1945. M18 crews did not remove conspicuous national insignia as readily as other American armoured vehicle crews; their vehicle, with its modern torsion bar suspension, more closely resembled German tanks.

106▲

107▲ 108▼

109. An M18 supporting the 63rd Division rolls down the autobahn outside Scheppach, Germany, 27 April 1945. This is a later production type with the muzzle brake.

110. An M18 of the 704th TD Battalion in the Lossnitz Forest, Germany, supporting the 89th Infantry Division, 5 May 1945.

111. The 637th TD Battalion was the only tank destroyer unit to see extensive combat in the Pacific using the M18 Hellcat.

▲109

▲110 ▼111

112▲

113▲   114▼

112. An M18 tank destroyer of the 637th TD Battalion supports the 37th Division during fighting in Baguio, Luzon, the Philippines, 24 April 1945.
113. An M18 of the 306th Anti-Tank Company of the 77th Division during fighting on Okinawa on 11 May 1945. Some infantry divisions in the final phases of the Pacific fighting were allotted self-propelled tank destroyers instead of the normal towed guns in their anti-tank companies.
114. An M18 of the 306th AT company firing at Japanese positions near Shuri, Okinawa, on 11 May 1945.

▲115

▲116 ▼117

115. This side view compares the M36 90mm GMC (right) with its ancestor, the M10 3in GMC. Both vehicles were externally almost identical except for the larger turret and gun of the M36. These two vehicles belong to the 703rd TD Battalion, and the photograph was taken when the M36 was first entering service in October 1944.

116. M36 crews train in France in October 1944 before being sent into action. By this stage, tank destroyer battalions were clamouring for a better armed vehicle to deal with German Panther and Tiger tanks. At first, M10 units were allocated small numbers of M36s, but battalions were formed entirely of these vehicles as the latter became available in greater numbers.

117. An M36 of the 607th Tank Destroyer Battalion in Metz on 20 November 1944. This battalion was equipped entirely with M36s.

118. Another view of an M36 of the 607th TD Battalion in Metz in November 1944.

119. An M36 of a tank destroyer battalion of Patton's Third Army is camouflaged with whitewash in Luxembourg on 3 January 1945 before being committed to the Ardennes fighting.

120. Another Third Army M36. The M36 was much prized in the Ardennes fighting as it was the only US armoured vehicle regularly capable of dealing with such German tanks as the Tiger or Panther.

118▲

119▲ 120▼

▲121

121. An M36 of the 703rd TD Battalion is helped out of a ditch near Manhay, Belgium, during the Ardennes fighting on 4 January 1945. This battalion was originally equipped with the M10.

122. The hefty shells for the 90mm gun of an M36 of the Third Army are loaded into the turret during a stop near Serrig, Germany, on 16 March 1945. The crewman to the right wears the Tank Destroyer Command insignia – an orange roundel containing a black panther crushing a tank in its teeth – on his shoulder.

123. An M36 of the 702nd TD Battalion, 2nd Armored Division, is helped back into position after skidding off a road near Fisennes, Belgium, 5 January 1945. Note the logs on the bow used to provide protection against German Panzerfaust anti-tank rockets.

124. An M36 of the 703rd TD Battalion passes a knocked-out German PzKpfw IV during the fighting near Langlir, Belgium, on 13 January 1945.

▼122

▲125

125. Troops of the 3rd Armored Division, with armoured 'doughs' in their M3A1 halftracks supported by an M36 tank destroyer, prepare to advance from the ruins of Duren, Germany, on 26 February 1945.

126. One of the more unusual tank destroyers used by the US Army in the Second World War was the M36B1. Instead of using the M10 hull, it utilized that of an M4A3 Sherman tank. This particular M36B1, serving with the 654th TD Battalion, was credited with knocking out two Tiger and two PzKpfw IV tanks and was photographed in Rheinberg, Germany, on 6 March 1945.

▼126

127▲

127. An M36 of the 899th TD Battalion in Bad Godesberg, Germany, on 7 March 1945. By the end of the war twenty-two tank destroyer battalions had either wholly or partially converted to the M36. The 899th TD Battalion had been among the original M10 units, first seeing action in North Africa in 1943.

128. An M36 supporting the 94th Division during fighting in Kell, Germany, on 15 March 1945.

128 ▼

129. An M36 waits for an ambulance for a wounded soldier while supporting the 71st Infantry Regiment near Guide Kirch, France, on 15 March 1945.

130. An M36 of the 691st TD Battalion on its way to the Königstein prisoner-of-war camp while attached to a 76th Division task force assigned to liberate the camp on 11 May 1945.

131. An M36 and an M2A1 halftrack of the 5th Armored Division fire against snipers in a tree-line. Note that the M36 has been fitted with a roof armour parapet.

132. After the war the M36 was finally modernized with overhead armour, being redesignated M36B2.

129▶

▼130

131▲ 132 ▼

133. By the time of the Korean War most M36s had been withdrawn from front-line US service. However, some were assigned to the Korean Army, like this M36 of the 53rd ROK Tank Company seen on 12 July 1952. The Koreans apparently appreciated the vulnerability of the open roof as had their American counterparts some five years earlier.

134. A recent incarnation of the tank destroyer concept is the M9 Hummer 5/4-ton truck TOW launch vehicle. A derivative of the M966 HMMWV 5/4-ton truck with light Kevlar armour in addition to its TOW anti-tank guided missile launcher, it will begin to enter US Army service in 1984. (AM General)

▲133 ▼134